MW01600567

All Rights Reserved.
Self Published in the United States
Edited by Nyndia Diligent-Jones
Original Story and Illustrations by Chase Jones
Book Design by Chase Jones

In loving memory
of my beautiful
Great-Grandmother Bee

You Will Always Be at Home in the Ocean

By Chase Jones

Off the coast in warm waters around the world is where octopuses live. They travel along the floor on the seabed. Using their eight long tentacles, the octopus walks along the rocks and coral looking for crabs to eat.

Octopus can have a fun time by changing the color of their skin to hide from other sea animals. They also like to pretend to be other sea animals, mirroring their shapes and gestures. If you'd like to meet an octopus, make sure to be friendly. Octopus are known for spraying ink in the faces of anyone being mean to them.

Octopuses are always looking for a new home as they travel around the seabed. They like to find an open hole in rocks, coral, caves, or any objects that can protect them from harm. They can find a home in empty clam shells and pretend to be a clam to surprise other animals.

Along the sea floor, among the rocks and coral is where the octopus calls home.

In every ocean on earth, you can find humpback whales. The humpbacks can be seen breathing air when they swim above the ocean water. These whales can grow over 60 feet long and weigh as much as 40 tons.

When you go diving into the ocean, you might hear a beautiful song. Humpbacks are known for the beautiful songs they sing to one another. It is believed to be a complex speech among the whales. These songs can go on for hours and can be heard from miles away.

The humpbacks travel each year during the summer near the North and South Poles. In the winter they travel back to the equator to mate. When a baby calf humpback is born, it stays with its mother until it is fully grown into an adult. As they travel around, they often touch fins while they swim. These whales swim close to coast lines to feed on schools of fish, krill, and plankton.

As one of the world's largest mammals, swimming in every ocean is where the humpback whale calls home.

There are more than 200 types of jellyfish floating in every ocean. Jellyfish are known for their special looking disk-shaped head and long tentacles. Their bodies are soft and made up of 99% water. They can be as little as one inch and as big as six feet.

The most common jellyfish are known to be free swimming animals that float near the shorelines around the world. One needs to be careful while swimming in these open waters.

Jellyfish have stinging cells on their tentacles used to catch their food. Every year people swim too close to jellyfish and have gotten stung. Even though it hurts remember that jellyfish are not mean animals!

Floating in deep dark oceans and the ocean shore is where the jellyfish calls home.

Did you know there are eight hundred different types of hermit crabs? Hermit crabs live in large groups of hundreds or more in the same area of the sea.

The hermit crab is not a relative of other crabs. They are more closely related to a lobster than a crab. Hermit crabs have a strong body, but a soft hook like tail that they need to protect. To protect their tails, the hermit crab will find empty seashells that can fit their tail and body in.

When hermit crabs discover a new shell, each crab will line up biggest to smallest. Each one will try on a new shell to find the next one that has room for them to grow. Just like people shopping in a clothing store, the hermit will try on different shells to find the best fit.

In beautiful seashells all around the world are where the hermit crab calls home.

Born in an egg buried deep under the warm sand are sea turtles. Throughout its life, a sea turtle returns to the same beach to lay 80 to 100 eggs underneath the sand.

The baby sea turtles are left to grow in these eggshells for 60 days. When the time comes, the babies hatch out of their shells and dig their way out of the sand.

Each baby sea turtle crawls on their bellies all the way to the sea water to be a part of the ocean. The babies find their way to the Gulf stream current in the Caribbean waters. The sea turtle floats among the seaweeds where there is plenty of food to help them grow.

Once the sea turtle is big and strong, they will return to the coast. Adult stay submerged in the ocean waters, floating around seaweed and coral where there is food for them.

In the warm Caribbean seas is where the sea turtle calls home.

In warm tropical waters around the world, you can find a tiny 'S' shaped animal. Seahorses have an 'S' shape body with a head like a horse. They can grow from less than an inch to 14 inches long. Seahorses can be found swimming among seaweed and coral. Using their tails, they wrap them around sea plants to stay anchored to eat. There are 25 known seahorses in the ocean.

The seahorse has an interesting way of swimming. They have fins to help them swim forward very slowly, but to move down they fill their bodies full of air. To move up, they slowly let out the air from their body.

Unlike most animals, the male seahorse carries the eggs and helps in their birth. The male has a small pouch on his belly to hold the eggs and protect them. After the babies are born, the seahorses stays together in a large group known as a herd.

In herds, tied to sea plants off the coastal shores is where the seahorse calls home.

In the tropics during the spring and summer, you can find the cuttlefish on the coastline.

A relative of octopuses and squids, the cuttlefish has eight tentacles extending from their flat body. Cuttlefish have an oblong shell shape head known as a cuttlebone. During the warm months of the year this fish is found in shallow waters. During the winter they swim out to deeper waters to mate.

The cuttlefish has two defenses against mean animals. If you come too close to a cuttlefish it will spray a cloud of ink and swim away very fast. The second is the cuttlefish can change the color of their skin and mimic the shapes of rocks, plants, and the seafloor. This is called camouflaging because they can hide in plain sight. The cuttlefish is beautiful and comes in many shapes and colors.

In the warm shallow waters is where the cuttlefish calls home.

Formerly known as a starfish is a creature that can be found in all sea waters around the world. Sea stars are not fish. They are more closely related to urchins and sea dollars than fish. With over 2,000 different types of sea stars, they are commonly known for their five arms.

Some sea stars can have 10, 20, or even 40 arms. Sea stars have bone tough like skin to protect them from other animals. The color of their skin also helps hide them among rocks and coral.

They have the amazing ability to regrow their broken arms, even some can grow a new body. With this ability, sea stars can live up to a full life of 35 years.

On the sea floor, among the rocks and coral is where sea star calls home.

These flatten disk like shape fish known as rays have long sharp spines for a tail. Stingrays are bottom dwellers, usually sticking close to the sea floor.

Sometimes they bury themselves in the sand. Rays live in large groups found in warmer waters near the tropics. They can defend themselves when threatened by whipping their sharp tails. The tail is strong enough to poke into the side of a boat.

There are about 534 different types of stingrays in the oceans. These rays are placed into four groups: electric rays, sawfish, skates, and stingrays.

At the bottom of the sea floor is where the ray fish calls home.

Many different types of fish travel in a large group in the ocean known as a school.

A school of fish is the same type of fish following a leader fish known as a robo-fish. There are different reasons for the school to form. Most common is defense from other hungry animals. Also coming together in a group can help the fish find and share food.

Did you know these fish have an organ on their skin that can feel the pressure in water change when other fish are near? Besides protection and food, the school of fish can find love. In these tightknit groups is where fish can find a mate.

Swimming next to all their friends is where a school of fish calls home.

In the freezing cold northern waters of the Artic, there lives a family of whales. The beluga and narwhal whales are closely related and look similar. However, there are some key differences between these whales. Narwhals are nicknamed 'the unicorn of the sea'. This whale has an enlarged tooth that can grow to 10 feet in length. It looks like a unicorn horn with its spiral shape. A Narwhal's body is a round shape unlike most other whales.

Beluga whales have white skin and have a round bump on their forehead. Belugas have a beautiful singing voice. They speak to each other by singing songs that are different from other whales and sea mammals. Both belugas and narwhals live in small groups of 10 to 20 in a pod. In the winter when the ice caps freeze over, they migrate in large groups to the coastline of Canada, Alaska, and Greenland.

Among the icebergs is where the beluga and narwhal calls home.

Living a very lonely life, the great hammerhead shark sticks to itself. The great hammerhead is the largest of these types of sharks.

Found in warm waters of 68 degrees or higher, the hammerhead travels far distances. Traveling as far as 800 miles in one trip! Their hammer shaped head helps the shark find it's food.

Spread out through the length of their head are electrical receptors. With these receptors, these sharks can find fish buried in the sand like the stingray. The hammerhead is immune to most stinging fish and usually eats these types of fish.

In the warm waters of the oceans, near the sand bed is where the great hammerhead calls home.

Growing no longer than 4 inches, the goby lives among the coral near the seashores. They prefer to live in warm tropical waters.

With a long jaw known as a mudsucker, these fish dig into the sand to build a den for protection. Sometimes they will have roommates like small shrimps and cleaner fish. The goby helps clean bigger fish when they swim by their den.

The cleaning of other fish feeds the goby, and the big fish gets a free bath. The goby fish like to live a quiet life.

Dug into the sand is where the goby calls home.

Among the coral off the coast of Asia and Australia is where you find the clown fish. There are over 20 different types of clown fish living in these warm waters.

Clown fish come in a variety of colors, but the most known is the orange and white clown fish. These fish live in anemones, a creature that is attached to the sea floor. Anemones have dozens of tentacles that have toxins for gathering food and protection. Over time, the clown fish has become immune to these toxins and lives within the tentacles.

Both the anemone and clown fish live with each other in friendship. All clown fish are born male, but around adulthood they can change to female. These fish live in a large group with one female for laying eggs.

Swimming in the tentacles of an anemone is where the clown fish calls home.

One type of mammal which lives in both rivers and seas, is the 'toothed whale' known as a dolphin. Of the 40 different types of dolphins, 6 are referred to as whales. The most common is an orca or the killer whale.

Dolphins are known for their crest moon shape, being very smart, and for their beautiful form of speaking. This form of speaking comes from sounds produced from ultrasonic pulses.

Dolphins are great swimmers, being able to reach speeds of 18 miles per hour. Dolphins travel in large groups with up to thousands in a single pod. This sea animal is very friendly to humans and likes to play around in the water. Dolphins are always spotted swimming along or behind boats, enjoying the waves the boats make.

Jumping out of the water into the sunset is where a dolphin calls home.

References

Augustyn, A. (2008, May 28). Octopus. Encyclopædia Britannica. Retrieved September 21, 2021, from https://www.britannica.com/animal/octopus-mollusk.

Boldlight. (2020, June 3). Narwhal: Unicorn of the sea. Whale & Dolphin Conservation USA. Retrieved September 21, 2021, from https://us.whales.org/whales-dolphins/species-guide/narwhal/.

Bradford, A. (2016, July 13). Facts about clownfish. LiveScience. Retrieved September 21, 2021, from https://www.livescience.com/55399-clownfish.html.

Carey, R. (n.d.). Seahorse. Animals. Retrieved September 21, 2021, from https://kids.nationalgeographic.com/animals/fish/facts/seahorse.

Chaddha, R. (2007, March). NOVA | kings of Camouflage | Anatomy of a Cuttlefish (non-Flash). PBS. Retrieved September 21, 2021, from https://www.pbs.org/wgbh/nova/camo/anat-nf.html.

Emily Brauner Author, Brauner, E., Author, Leonard, G., Mallos, N., Spencer, E., & Browder, K. (2018, September 7). Fish 101: Back to school. Ocean Conservancy. Retrieved September 21, 2021, from https://oceanconservancy.org/blog/2018/09/07/fish-101-back-school/.

Lotha, G. (1998, July 20). jellyfish. Encyclopædia Britannica. Retrieved September 21, 2021, from https://www.britannica.com/animal/jellyfish.

Lotha, G. (2006, September 29). Dolphin. Encyclopædia Britannica. Retrieved September 21, 2021, from https://www.britannica.com/animal/dolphin-mammal.

Lotha, G. (2008, June 17). Goby. Encyclopædia Britannica. Retrieved September 21, 2021, from https://www.britannica.com/animal/goby.

Nicklen, P. (n.d.). Humpback whale: National geographic. Animals. Retrieved September 21, 2021, from https://www.nationalgeographic.com/animals/mammals/facts/humpback-whale.

Rafferty, J. P. (2006, October 16). Cuttlefish. Encyclopædia Britannica. Retrieved September 21, 2021, from https://www.britannica.com/animal/cuttlefish.

Rodriguez, E. (2006, May 26). ray. Encyclopædia Britannica. Retrieved September 21, 2021, from https://www.britannica.com/animal/ray-fish.

Rodriguez, E. (2008, August 29). Stingray. Encyclopædia Britannica. Retrieved September 21, 2021, from https://www.britannica.com/animal/stingray.

Sartore, J. (n.d.). Hermit crabs, facts and photos. Animals. Retrieved September 21, 2021, from https://www.nationalgeographic.com/animals/invertebrates/-facts/hermit-crabs.

Sartore, J. (n.d.). Starfish (sea Stars): National Geographic. Animals. Retrieved September 21, 2021, from https://www.nationalgeographic.com/animals/invertebrates/facts/starfish-1.

Sea Turtle Conservancy. (n.d.). Information About Sea Turtles: General Behavior. conserveturtles.org. Retrieved September 21, 2021, from https://conserveturtles.org/information-sea-turtles-general-behavior/.

About the Author

Chase Jones was born in
Denver, Colorado. He attended Colorado
State University and received a bachelor's
in history.

After college he spent two years on
the Island of Dominica
as a Peace Corps Volunteer.

He eventually moved to
New York City and worked at the
Metropolitan Museum of Art.

Chase and his wife, Nyndia,
a designer/fiber artist
now live in Boston, MA.

Made in the USA
Middletown, DE
24 November 2025

21745721R10022